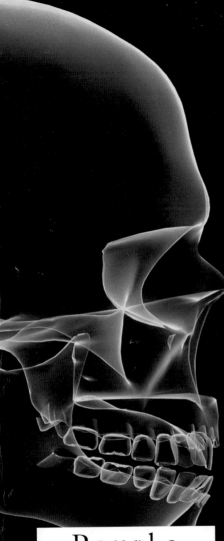

Why Do I Have Bones?

Jo Cleland

Rourke
Publishing LLC
Vero Beach, Florida 32964

This book can be sung to the tune of "The Hokey Pokey."

www.rourkepublishing.com

PHOTO CREDITS: Title Page: © Martin Garnham; page 3: © Aaliya Landholt, © Bart Broek; page 4: © Linda Bucklin; page 5: © Renee Brady; page 6: © Coletti Daniele; page 7: © Renee Brady; page 8: © Harun Aydin; page 9: © Andrew Manley; page 10: © Renee Brady; page 12: © Michael Krinke, © Aaliya Landholt; page 13: © Andrea Gingerich; page 14: © Linda Bucklin; page 15: © Cindy Minear; page 16: © Robert Kudera; page 17: © Jaren Wicklund; page 18: © Coletti Daniele; page 19: © Linda Bucklin; page 20: © angelhell; page 21: © Bonnie Jacobs

Editor: Kelli L. Hicks

Cover design by: Nicola Stratford: bdpublishing.com

Interior design by: Renee Brady

Library of Congress Cataloging-in-Publication Data

Cleland, Joann
   Why do I have bones? / Jo Cleland.
      p. cm. -- (My first science library)
   ISBN 978-1-60472-540-7
   1. Bones--Juvenile literature. I. Title.
   QP88.2.C542 2009
   612.7'5--dc22

                              2008027362

Printed in the USA

CG/CG

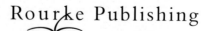

Rourke Publishing

www.rourkepublishing.com – rourke@rourkepublishing.com
Post Office Box 3328, Vero Beach, FL 32964

I have bones in my hands.

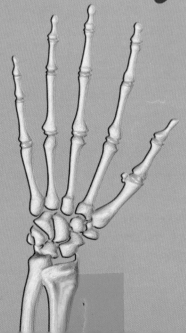

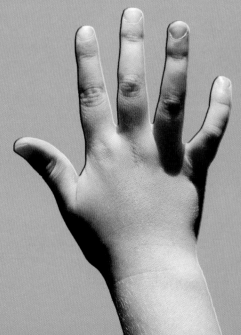

I have bones in my legs.

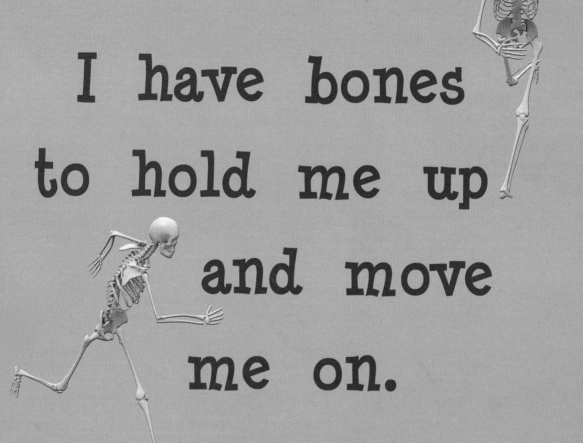

I have bones
to hold me up
and move
me on.

I have bones in my chest. I have bones in my head.

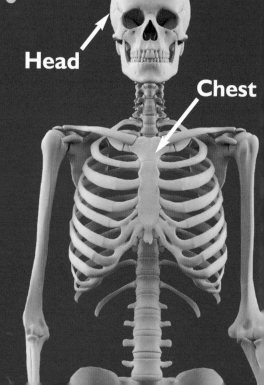

Head

Chest

Bones keep me safe when things go wrong.

I have bones in my feet.

I have bones in my arm.

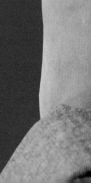
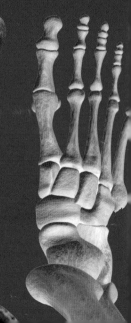

13

Some bones are short and some are long.

15

I have bones in

my jaw.

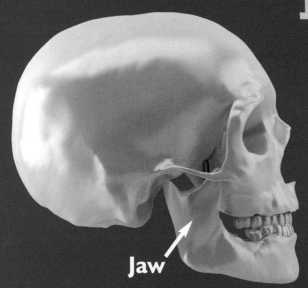

Jaw

I have bones EVERYWHERE!

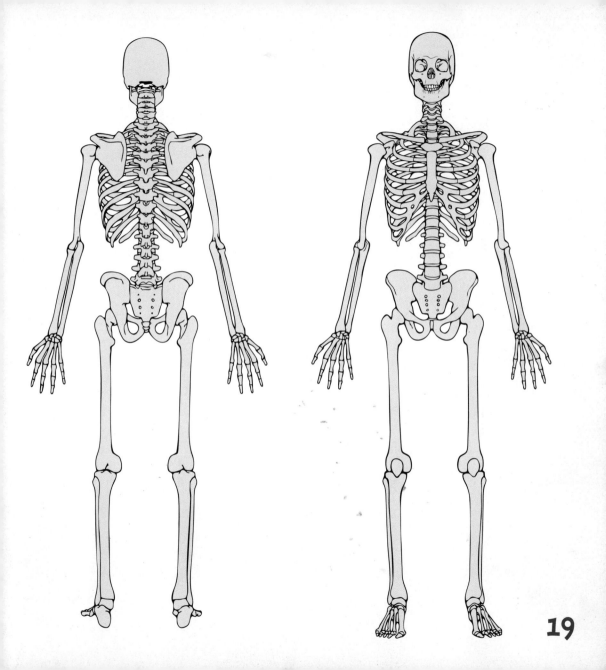

19

Bones help
to keep
me strong.

Glossary

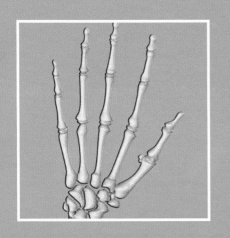

bones (BOHNZ): The hard, white parts that make up the skeleton of a person or animal. Most people have 206 bones.

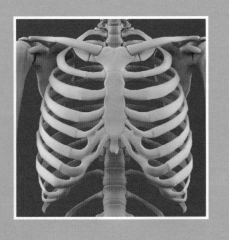

chest (CHEST): The chest is the front part of your body between your neck and your belly. The bones in your chest are called the sternum and the ribs.

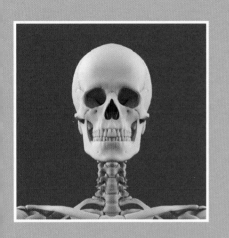

head (HED): The top part of your body attached to your neck. Your brain is inside your head. The bones in your head are called the skull.

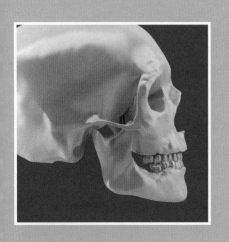

jaw (JAW): Your jaw is the lower part of your face that moves when you open your mouth. The jawbone, called the mandible, is part of your skull.

Index

Further Reading

Balestrino, Philip. *The Skeleton Inside You*. HarperCollins, 1989.

Novak, Micahel. *The Glow-In-The-Dark Book of the Human Skeletons*. Random House, 1997.

Thames, Susan. *Our Skeleton*. Rourke, 2008.

Websites

http://www.childrensmuseum.org/special_exhibits/bones/ kids_mazeGame.htm

http://wellnessways.aces.uiuc.edu/coloringbook/funactivities.html

http://www.medtropolis.com/VBody.asp

About the Authors

Jo Cleland loves to write books, compose songs, and make games. She loves to read, sing, and play games with children.